WHERE ARE YOU, GOD?
PSALM 139 FOR CHILDREN

BY ELSPETH CAMPBELL MURPHY
ILLUSTRATED BY JANE E. NELSON

Chariot Books

WHERE ARE YOU, GOD?
PSALM 139 FOR CHILDREN

Oh, God, you know all about me. You know
everything I do.

You see me when I run and when I rest.

You even know what I'm thinking. And you know what I'm going to say before I say it.

You knew all about me before I was born. You knew me when I was just a little baby. And you'll still know me when I'm all grown-up.

Though I can't see you, I know you are all around me. You are in front of me and behind me. You are everywhere! Is there anyplace I could go and you wouldn't be there?

If I had wings like a bird and could fly as high and as far as the morning sun, you would still be there.

If I had fins like a fish and could swim deep, deep to the bottom of the ocean, you would still be there. You are with me wherever I go.

But sometimes at night, when I'm alone in my room and everything is dark, I'm afraid you won't see me.

Then I remember that the dark doesn't matter to
you. You can still *see* me. And all through the night you
take good care of me.

And then in the morning I wake up and smile, because I know you are still here, and I am still with you.

Oh, God, you know all about me. You know about everything I do. Show me if I do anything that makes you sad.
And help me to love you forever.